SITTING WELL AT THE WELL 30-DAY JOURNAL

Sitting Well At The Well Collection

Dr. Jeanne Brooks

Elani
PUBLISHING
A PRINT, DIGITAL & TECHNOLOGY COMPANY

For information contact :

http://www.drjeannebrooks.com

Book and Cover design by Anika Janelle Pettiford

ISBN-13: 978-1985574601

ISBN-10: 1985574608

DAY ONE
SITTING WELL AT THE WELL

Satan's Lies   *God's Truths*

_____   _____

_____   _____

_____   _____

_____   _____

_____   _____

Defense Strategies

Positioning Yourself by pursuing God's Will

Who – Who is God using in my life?

_____

_____

What – What is God doing around me?

_____

_____

Where – Where do I see God most evident?

_____

_____

When – When do I feel most filled with the Fruits of the Spirit; peace, joy, love, gentleness, kindness, goodness, self-control, patience, and faithfulness

_____

_____

Armor of God

Armor Yourself

Belt of Truth - The truths God has revealed to me today

_____

_____

Breastplate of Righteousness – How has the Blood of Christ washed me clean?

_____

_____

Shoes of Peace – How has God reminded me that the battle is won?

_____

_____

Shield of Faith – How has God, in the past, rose beauty from ashes and restored what the locusts have eaten?

_____

_____

Helmet of Salvation – Who did Christ die for?

_____

_____

Sword of the Spirit – What verses or Bible stories has the Holy Spirit brought to mind to cut through the lies?

_____

_____

Prayer – My prayer today

_____

_____

_____

_____

God is a God of balance
Balance yourself

Spiritual – Today I will_____ to grow closer to God.

Mental – Today I will set my thoughts on_____.

Emotional – Today I will not be anxious about_____, but focus on_____.

Physical – Today I will treat my body as a temple by_____.

Social – Today I will edify the body of Christ by_____.

DAY TWO
SITTING WELL AT THE WELL

Satan's Lies	*God's Truths*
_____	_____
_____	_____
_____	_____
_____	_____
_____	_____

Defense Strategies

Positioning Yourself by pursuing God's Will

Who – Who is God using in my life?

_____

_____

What – What is God doing around me?

_____

_____

Where – Where do I see God most evident?

_____

_____

When – When do I feel most filled with the Fruits of the Spirit; peace, joy, love, gentleness, kindness, goodness, self-control, patience, and faithfulness

_____

_____

Armor of God

Armor Yourself

Belt of Truth - The truths God has revealed to me today

_____

_____

Breastplate of Righteousness – How has the Blood of Christ washed me clean?

_____

Shoes of Peace – How has God reminded me that the battle is won?

_____

Shield of Faith – How has God, in the past, rose beauty from ashes and restored what the locusts have eaten?

_____

Helmet of Salvation – Who did Christ die for?

_____

Sword of the Spirit – What verses or Bible stories has the Holy Spirit brought to mind to cut through the lies?

_____

_____

Prayer – My prayer today

_____

_____

_____

_____

God is a God of balance

Balance yourself

Spiritual – Today I will_____ to grow closer to God.

Mental – Today I will set my thoughts on_____.

Emotional – Today I will not be anxious about_____, but focus on_____.

Physical – Today I will treat my body as a temple by_____.

Social – Today I will edify the body of Christ by_____.

* * *

DAY THREE

SITTING WELL AT THE WELL

Satan's Lies	*God's Truths*
_____	_____
_____	_____
_____	_____
_____	_____
_____	_____

Defense Strategies

Positioning Yourself by pursuing God's Will

Who – Who is God using in my life?

_____

_____

What – What is God doing around me?

_____

_____

Where – Where do I see God most evident?

_____

_____

When – When do I feel most filled with the Fruits of the Spirit; peace, joy, love, gentleness, kindness, goodness, self-control, patience, and faithfulness

_____

_____

Armor of God

Armor Yourself

Belt of Truth - The truths God has revealed to me today

_____

Breastplate of Righteousness – How has the Blood of Christ washed me clean?

_____

_____

Shoes of Peace – How has God reminded me that the battle is won?

_____

_____

Shield of Faith – How has God, in the past, rose beauty from ashes and restored what the locusts have eaten?

_____

_____

Helmet of Salvation – Who did Christ die for?

_____

_____

Sword of the Spirit – What verses or Bible stories has the Holy Spirit brought to mind to cut through the lies?

_____

_____

Prayer – My prayer today

_____

_____

_____

_____

God is a God of balance
Balance yourself

Spiritual – Today I will_____ to grow closer to God.

Mental – Today I will set my thoughts on_____.

Emotional – Today I will not be anxious about_____, but focus

on_____.

Physical – Today I will treat my body as a temple by_____.

Social – Today I will edify the body of Christ

by_____.

***

DAY FOUR
SITTING WELL AT THE WELL

Satan's Lies	*God's Truths*
_____	_____
_____	_____
_____	_____
_____	_____
_____	_____

Defense Strategies

Positioning Yourself by pursuing God's Will

Who – Who is God using in my life?

_____
_____

What – What is God doing around me?

_____
_____

Where – Where do I see God most evident?

_____
_____

When – When do I feel most filled with the Fruits of the Spirit; peace, joy, love, gentleness, kindness, goodness, self-control, patience, and faithfulness

_____
_____

Armor of God

Armor Yourself

Belt of Truth - The truths God has revealed to me today

_____

Breastplate of Righteousness – How has the Blood of Christ washed me clean?

_____

_____

Shoes of Peace – How has God reminded me that the battle is won?

_____

_____

Shield of Faith – How has God, in the past, rose beauty from ashes and restored what the locusts have eaten?

_____

_____

Helmet of Salvation – Who did Christ die for?

_____

_____

Sword of the Spirit – What verses or Bible stories has the Holy Spirit brought to mind to cut through the lies?

_____

_____

Prayer – My prayer today

_____

_____

_____

_____

God is a God of balance
Balance yourself

Spiritual – Today I will_____ to grow closer to God.

Mental – Today I will set my thoughts on_____.

Emotional – Today I will not be anxious about_____, but focus

on_____.

Physical – Today I will treat my body as a temple by_____.

Social – Today I will edify the body of Christ

by_____.

* * *

DAY FIVE
SITTING WELL AT THE WELL

Satan's Lies   *God's Truths*

_____   _____
_____   _____
_____   _____
_____   _____
_____   _____

Defense Strategies
Positioning Yourself by pursuing God's Will

Who – Who is God using in my life?
_____
_____

What – What is God doing around me?
_____
_____

Where – Where do I see God most evident?
_____
_____

When – When do I feel most filled with the Fruits of the Spirit; peace, joy, love, gentleness, kindness, goodness, self-control, patience, and faithfulness
_____
_____

Armor of God
Armor Yourself

Belt of Truth - The truths God has revealed to me today
_____

Breastplate of Righteousness – How has the Blood of Christ washed me clean?

_____

_____

Shoes of Peace – How has God reminded me that the battle is won?

_____

_____

Shield of Faith – How has God, in the past, rose beauty from ashes and restored what the locusts have eaten?

_____

_____

Helmet of Salvation – Who did Christ die for?

_____

_____

Sword of the Spirit – What verses or Bible stories has the Holy Spirit brought to mind to cut through the lies?

_____

_____

Prayer – My prayer today

_____

_____

_____

_____

God is a God of balance
Balance yourself

Spiritual – Today I will_____ to grow closer to God.

Mental – Today I will set my thoughts on_____.

Emotional – Today I will not be anxious about_____, but focus on_____.

Physical – Today I will treat my body as a temple by_____.

Social – Today I will edify the body of Christ

by_____.

DAY SIX
SITTING WELL AT THE WELL

Satan's Lies   *God's Truths*

_____   _____
_____   _____
_____   _____
_____   _____
_____   _____

Defense Strategies
Positioning Yourself by pursuing God's Will

Who – Who is God using in my life?

_____

_____

What – What is God doing around me?

_____

_____

Where – Where do I see God most evident?

_____

_____

When – When do I feel most filled with the Fruits of the Spirit; peace, joy, love, gentleness, kindness, goodness, self-control, patience, and faithfulness

_____

_____

Armor of God
Armor Yourself

Belt of Truth - The truths God has revealed to me today

_____

_____

Breastplate of Righteousness – How has the Blood of Christ washed me clean?

_____

_____

Shoes of Peace – How has God reminded me that the battle is won?

_____

_____

Shield of Faith – How has God, in the past, rose beauty from ashes and restored what the locusts have eaten?

_____

_____

Helmet of Salvation – Who did Christ die for?

_____

_____

Sword of the Spirit – What verses or Bible stories has the Holy Spirit brought to mind to cut through the lies?

_____

_____

Prayer – My prayer today

_____

_____

_____

_____

God is a God of balance
Balance yourself

Spiritual – Today I will_____ to grow closer to God.

Mental – Today I will set my thoughts on_____.

Emotional – Today I will not be anxious about_____, but focus

on_____.

Physical – Today I will treat my body as a temple by_____.

Social – Today I will edify the body of Christ

by_____.

* * *

DAY SEVEN

SITTING WELL AT THE WELL

Satan's Lies	*God's Truths*
_____	_____
_____	_____
_____	_____
_____	_____
_____	_____

Defense Strategies

Positioning Yourself by pursuing God's Will

Who – Who is God using in my life?

_____

_____

What – What is God doing around me?

_____

_____

Where – Where do I see God most evident?

_____

_____

When – When do I feel most filled with the Fruits of the Spirit; peace, joy, love, gentleness, kindness, goodness, self-control, patience, and faithfulness

_____

_____

Armor of God

Armor Yourself

Belt of Truth - The truths God has revealed to me today

_____

_____

Breastplate of Righteousness – How has the Blood of Christ washed me clean?

_____

_____

Shoes of Peace – How has God reminded me that the battle is won?

_____

_____

Shield of Faith – How has God, in the past, rose beauty from ashes and restored what the locusts have eaten?

_____

_____

Helmet of Salvation – Who did Christ die for?

_____

_____

Sword of the Spirit – What verses or Bible stories has the Holy Spirit brought to mind to cut through the lies?

_____

_____

Prayer – My prayer today

_____

_____

_____

_____

God is a God of balance
Balance yourself

Spiritual – Today I will_____ to grow closer to God.

Mental – Today I will set my thoughts on_____.

Emotional – Today I will not be anxious about_____, but focus on_____.

Physical – Today I will treat my body as a temple by_____.

Social – Today I will edify the body of Christ by_____.

DAY EIGHT

SITTING WELL AT THE WELL

Satan's Lies	*God's Truths*
_____	_____
_____	_____
_____	_____
_____	_____
_____	_____

Defense Strategies

Positioning Yourself by pursuing God's Will

Who – Who is God using in my life?

_____

_____

What – What is God doing around me?

_____

_____

Where – Where do I see God most evident?

_____

_____

When – When do I feel most filled with the Fruits of the Spirit; peace, joy, love, gentleness, kindness, goodness, self-control, patience, and faithfulness

_____

_____

Armor of God

Armor Yourself

Belt of Truth - The truths God has revealed to me today

_____

_____

Breastplate of Righteousness – How has the Blood of Christ washed me clean?

_____

_____

Shoes of Peace – How has God reminded me that the battle is won?

_____

_____

Shield of Faith – How has God, in the past, rose beauty from ashes and restored what the locusts have eaten?

_____

_____

Helmet of Salvation – Who did Christ die for?

_____

_____

Sword of the Spirit – What verses or Bible stories has the Holy Spirit brought to mind to cut through the lies?

_____

_____

Prayer – My prayer today

_____

_____

_____

_____

God is a God of balance

Balance yourself

Spiritual – Today I will_____ to grow closer to God.

Mental – Today I will set my thoughts on_____.

Emotional – Today I will not be anxious about_____, but focus

on_____.

Physical – Today I will treat my body as a temple by_____.

Social – Today I will edify the body of Christ

by_____.

DR. JEANNE BROOKS

* * *

DAY NINE
SITTING WELL AT THE WELL

Satan's Lies   *God's Truths*

_____   _____

_____   _____

_____   _____

_____   _____

_____   _____

Defense Strategies

Positioning Yourself by pursuing God's Will

Who – Who is God using in my life?

_____

_____

What – What is God doing around me?

_____

_____

Where – Where do I see God most evident?

_____

_____

When – When do I feel most filled with the Fruits of the Spirit; peace, joy, love, gentleness, kindness, goodness, self-control, patience, and faithfulness

_____

_____

Armor of God

Armor Yourself

Belt of Truth - The truths God has revealed to me today

_____

Breastplate of Righteousness – How has the Blood of Christ washed me clean?

_____

_____

Shoes of Peace – How has God reminded me that the battle is won?

_____

_____

Shield of Faith – How has God, in the past, rose beauty from ashes and restored what the locusts have eaten?

_____

_____

Helmet of Salvation – Who did Christ die for?

_____

_____

Sword of the Spirit – What verses or Bible stories has the Holy Spirit brought to mind to cut through the lies?

_____

_____

Prayer – My prayer today

_____

_____

_____

_____

God is a God of balance
Balance yourself

Spiritual – Today I will_____ to grow closer to God.

Mental – Today I will set my thoughts on_____.

Emotional – Today I will not be anxious about_____, but focus

on_____.

Physical – Today I will treat my body as a temple by_____.

Social – Today I will edify the body of Christ

by_____.

DAY TEN
SITTING WELL AT THE WELL

Satan's Lies   *God's Truths*

_____   _____
_____   _____
_____   _____
_____   _____
_____   _____

Defense Strategies
Positioning Yourself by pursuing God's Will

Who – Who is God using in my life?
_____
_____

What – What is God doing around me?
_____
_____

Where – Where do I see God most evident?
_____
_____

When – When do I feel most filled with the Fruits of the Spirit; peace, joy, love, gentleness, kindness, goodness, self-control, patience, and faithfulness
_____
_____

Armor of God
Armor Yourself

Belt of Truth - The truths God has revealed to me today
_____

_____

Breastplate of Righteousness – How has the Blood of Christ washed me clean?

_____

_____

Shoes of Peace – How has God reminded me that the battle is won?

_____

_____

Shield of Faith – How has God, in the past, rose beauty from ashes and restored what the locusts have eaten?

_____

_____

Helmet of Salvation – Who did Christ die for?

_____

_____

Sword of the Spirit – What verses or Bible stories has the Holy Spirit brought to mind to cut through the lies?

_____

_____

Prayer – My prayer today

_____

_____

_____

_____

God is a God of balance
Balance yourself

Spiritual – Today I will_____ to grow closer to God.

Mental – Today I will set my thoughts on_____.

Emotional – Today I will not be anxious about_____, but focus on_____.

Physical – Today I will treat my body as a temple by_____.

Social – Today I will edify the body of Christ by_____.

* * *

DAY ELEVEN
SITTING WELL AT THE WELL

Satan's Lies   *God's Truths*

_____   _____
_____   _____
_____   _____
_____   _____
_____

Defense Strategies
Positioning Yourself by pursuing God's Will

Who – Who is God using in my life?

What – What is God doing around me?

Where – Where do I see God most evident?

When – When do I feel most filled with the Fruits of the Spirit; peace, joy, love, gentleness, kindness, goodness, self-control, patience, and faithfulness

Armor of God
Armor Yourself

Belt of Truth - The truths God has revealed to me today

Breastplate of Righteousness – How has the Blood of Christ washed me clean?

_____

_____

Shoes of Peace – How has God reminded me that the battle is won?

_____

_____

Shield of Faith – How has God, in the past, rose beauty from ashes and restored what the locusts have eaten?

_____

_____

Helmet of Salvation – Who did Christ die for?

_____

_____

Sword of the Spirit – What verses or Bible stories has the Holy Spirit brought to mind to cut through the lies?

_____

_____

Prayer – My prayer today

_____

_____

_____

_____

God is a God of balance
Balance yourself

Spiritual – Today I will_____ to grow closer to God.

Mental – Today I will set my thoughts on_____.

Emotional – Today I will not be anxious about_____, but focus on_____.

Physical – Today I will treat my body as a temple by_____.

Social – Today I will edify the body of Christ by_____.

DAY TWELVE
SITTING WELL AT THE WELL

Satan's Lies	*God's Truths*
_____	_____
_____	_____
_____	_____
_____	_____
_____	_____

Defense Strategies

Positioning Yourself by pursuing God's Will

Who – Who is God using in my life?

_____

_____

What – What is God doing around me?

_____

_____

Where – Where do I see God most evident?

_____

_____

When – When do I feel most filled with the Fruits of the Spirit; peace, joy, love, gentleness, kindness, goodness, self-control, patience, and faithfulness

_____

_____

Armor of God

Armor Yourself

Belt of Truth - The truths God has revealed to me today

_____

Breastplate of Righteousness – How has the Blood of Christ washed me clean?

_____

_____

Shoes of Peace – How has God reminded me that the battle is won?

_____

_____

Shield of Faith – How has God, in the past, rose beauty from ashes and restored what the locusts have eaten?

_____

_____

Helmet of Salvation – Who did Christ die for?

_____

_____

Sword of the Spirit – What verses or Bible stories has the Holy Spirit brought to mind to cut through the lies?

_____

_____

Prayer – My prayer today

_____

_____

_____

_____

God is a God of balance
Balance yourself

Spiritual – Today I will_____ to grow closer to God.

Mental – Today I will set my thoughts on_____.

Emotional – Today I will not be anxious about_____, but focus on_____.

Physical – Today I will treat my body as a temple by_____.

Social – Today I will edify the body of Christ

by_____.

* * *

DAY THIRTEEN
SITTING WELL AT THE WELL

Satan's Lies   *God's Truths*

_____	_____
_____	_____
_____	_____
_____	_____
_____	_____

Defense Strategies
Positioning Yourself by pursuing God's Will

Who – Who is God using in my life?

What – What is God doing around me?

Where – Where do I see God most evident?

When – When do I feel most filled with the Fruits of the Spirit; peace, joy, love, gentleness, kindness, goodness, self-control, patience, and faithfulness

Armor of God
Armor Yourself

Belt of Truth - The truths God has revealed to me today

Breastplate of Righteousness – How has the Blood of Christ washed me clean?

_____

_____

Shoes of Peace – How has God reminded me that the battle is won?

_____

_____

Shield of Faith – How has God, in the past, rose beauty from ashes and restored what the locusts have eaten?

_____

_____

Helmet of Salvation – Who did Christ die for?

_____

_____

Sword of the Spirit – What verses or Bible stories has the Holy Spirit brought to mind to cut through the lies?

_____

_____

Prayer – My prayer today

_____

_____

_____

_____

God is a God of balance
Balance yourself

Spiritual – Today I will_____ to grow closer to God.

Mental – Today I will set my thoughts on_____.

Emotional – Today I will not be anxious about_____, but focus on_____.

Physical – Today I will treat my body as a temple by_____.

Social – Today I will edify the body of Christ by_____.

DAY FOURTEEN
SITTING WELL AT THE WELL

Satan's Lies	*God's Truths*
_____	_____
_____	_____
_____	_____
_____	_____

Defense Strategies

Positioning Yourself by pursuing God's Will

Who – Who is God using in my life?

_____

_____

What – What is God doing around me?

_____

_____

Where – Where do I see God most evident?

_____

_____

When – When do I feel most filled with the Fruits of the Spirit; peace, joy, love, gentleness, kindness, goodness, self-control, patience, and faithfulness

_____

_____

Armor of God

Armor Yourself

Belt of Truth - The truths God has revealed to me today

_____

_____

Breastplate of Righteousness – How has the Blood of Christ washed me clean?

_____

_____

Shoes of Peace – How has God reminded me that the battle is won?

_____

_____

Shield of Faith – How has God, in the past, rose beauty from ashes and restored what the locusts have eaten?

_____

_____

Helmet of Salvation – Who did Christ die for?

_____

_____

Sword of the Spirit – What verses or Bible stories has the Holy Spirit brought to mind to cut through the lies?

_____

_____

Prayer – My prayer today

_____

_____

_____

_____

God is a God of balance
Balance yourself

Spiritual – Today I will_____ to grow closer to God.

Mental – Today I will set my thoughts on_____.

Emotional – Today I will not be anxious about_____, but focus

on_____.

Physical – Today I will treat my body as a temple by_____.

Social – Today I will edify the body of Christ

by_____.

* * *

DAY FIFTEEN
SITTING WELL AT THE WELL

Satan's Lies	*God's Truths*
_____	_____
_____	_____
_____	_____
_____	_____
_____	_____

Defense Strategies

Positioning Yourself by pursuing God's Will

Who – Who is God using in my life?

_____

_____

What – What is God doing around me?

_____

_____

Where – Where do I see God most evident?

_____

_____

When – When do I feel most filled with the Fruits of the Spirit; peace, joy, love, gentleness, kindness, goodness, self-control, patience, and faithfulness

_____

_____

Armor of God

Armor Yourself

Belt of Truth - The truths God has revealed to me today

_____

_____

Breastplate of Righteousness – How has the Blood of Christ washed me clean?

_____

_____

Shoes of Peace – How has God reminded me that the battle is won?

_____

_____

Shield of Faith – How has God, in the past, rose beauty from ashes and restored what the locusts have eaten?

_____

_____

Helmet of Salvation – Who did Christ die for?

_____

_____

Sword of the Spirit – What verses or Bible stories has the Holy Spirit brought to mind to cut through the lies?

_____

_____

Prayer – My prayer today

_____

_____

_____

_____

God is a God of balance

Balance yourself

Spiritual – Today I will_____ to grow closer to God.

Mental – Today I will set my thoughts on_____.

Emotional – Today I will not be anxious about_____, but focus on_____.

Physical – Today I will treat my body as a temple by_____.

Social – Today I will edify the body of Christ by_____.

DAY SIXTEEN
SITTING WELL AT THE WELL

Satan's Lies	*God's Truths*
_____	_____
_____	_____
_____	_____
_____	_____
_____	_____

Defense Strategies

Positioning Yourself by pursuing God's Will

Who – Who is God using in my life?

_____

What – What is God doing around me?

_____

Where – Where do I see God most evident?

_____

When – When do I feel most filled with the Fruits of the Spirit; peace, joy, love, gentleness, kindness, goodness, self-control, patience, and faithfulness

_____

_____

Armor of God

Armor Yourself

Belt of Truth - The truths God has revealed to me today

_____

_____

Breastplate of Righteousness – How has the Blood of Christ washed me clean?

_____

_____

Shoes of Peace – How has God reminded me that the battle is won?

_____

_____

Shield of Faith – How has God, in the past, rose beauty from ashes and restored what the locusts have eaten?

_____

_____

Helmet of Salvation – Who did Christ die for?

_____

_____

Sword of the Spirit – What verses or Bible stories has the Holy Spirit brought to mind to cut through the lies?

_____

_____

Prayer – My prayer today

_____

_____

_____

_____

God is a God of balance
Balance yourself

Spiritual – Today I will_____ to grow closer to God.

Mental – Today I will set my thoughts on_____.

Emotional – Today I will not be anxious about_____, but focus on_____.

Physical – Today I will treat my body as a temple by_____.

Social – Today I will edify the body of Christ by_____.

DR. JEANNE BROOKS

* * *

DAY SEVENTEEN
SITTING WELL AT THE WELL

<table>
<tr><td>*Satan's Lies*</td><td>*God's Truths*</td></tr>
<tr><td>_____</td><td>_____</td></tr>
<tr><td>_____</td><td>_____</td></tr>
<tr><td>_____</td><td>_____</td></tr>
<tr><td>_____</td><td>_____</td></tr>
<tr><td>_____</td><td>_____</td></tr>
</table>

Defense Strategies
Positioning Yourself by pursuing God's Will

Who – Who is God using in my life?

_____

_____

What – What is God doing around me?

_____

_____

Where – Where do I see God most evident?

_____

_____

When – When do I feel most filled with the Fruits of the Spirit; peace, joy, love, gentleness, kindness, goodness, self-control, patience, and faithfulness

_____

_____

Armor of God
Armor Yourself

Belt of Truth - The truths God has revealed to me today

_____

_____

Breastplate of Righteousness – How has the Blood of Christ washed me clean?

_____

_____

Shoes of Peace – How has God reminded me that the battle is won?

_____

_____

Shield of Faith – How has God, in the past, rose beauty from ashes and restored what the locusts have eaten?

_____

_____

Helmet of Salvation – Who did Christ die for?

_____

_____

Sword of the Spirit – What verses or Bible stories has the Holy Spirit brought to mind to cut through the lies?

_____

_____

Prayer – My prayer today

_____

_____

_____

_____

God is a God of balance

Balance yourself

Spiritual – Today I will_____ to grow closer to God.

Mental – Today I will set my thoughts on_____.

Emotional – Today I will not be anxious about_____, but focus

on_____.

Physical – Today I will treat my body as a temple by_____.

Social – Today I will edify the body of Christ

by_____.

DAY EIGHTEEN
SITTING WELL AT THE WELL

Satan's Lies   *God's Truths*

_____   _____
_____   _____
_____   _____
_____   _____
_____   _____

Defense Strategies

Positioning Yourself by pursuing God's Will

Who – Who is God using in my life?

_____

_____

What – What is God doing around me?

_____

_____

Where – Where do I see God most evident?

_____

_____

When – When do I feel most filled with the Fruits of the Spirit; peace, joy, love, gentleness, kindness, goodness, self-control, patience, and faithfulness

_____

_____

Armor of God

Armor Yourself

Belt of Truth - The truths God has revealed to me today

_____

_____

Breastplate of Righteousness – How has the Blood of Christ washed me clean?

_____

_____

Shoes of Peace – How has God reminded me that the battle is won?

_____

_____

Shield of Faith – How has God, in the past, rose beauty from ashes and restored what the locusts have eaten?

_____

_____

Helmet of Salvation – Who did Christ die for?

_____

_____

Sword of the Spirit – What verses or Bible stories has the Holy Spirit brought to mind to cut through the lies?

_____

_____

Prayer – My prayer today

_____

_____

_____

_____

God is a God of balance

Balance yourself

Spiritual – Today I will_____ to grow closer to God.

Mental – Today I will set my thoughts on_____.

Emotional – Today I will not be anxious about_____, but focus

on_____.

Physical – Today I will treat my body as a temple by_____.

Social – Today I will edify the body of Christ

by_____.

DR. JEANNE BROOKS

* * *

DAY NINETEEN
SITTING WELL AT THE WELL

Satan's Lies   *God's Truths*

_____   _____
_____   _____
_____   _____
_____   _____
_____   _____

Defense Strategies

Positioning Yourself by pursuing God's Will

Who – Who is God using in my life?

_____

_____

What – What is God doing around me?

_____

_____

Where – Where do I see God most evident?

_____

_____

When – When do I feel most filled with the Fruits of the Spirit; peace, joy, love, gentleness, kindness, goodness, self-control, patience, and faithfulness

_____

_____

Armor of God

Armor Yourself

Belt of Truth - The truths God has revealed to me today

_____

_____

Breastplate of Righteousness – How has the Blood of Christ washed me clean?

_____

_____

Shoes of Peace – How has God reminded me that the battle is won?

_____

_____

Shield of Faith – How has God, in the past, rose beauty from ashes and restored what the locusts have eaten?

_____

_____

Helmet of Salvation – Who did Christ die for?

_____

_____

Sword of the Spirit – What verses or Bible stories has the Holy Spirit brought to mind to cut through the lies?

_____

_____

Prayer – My prayer today

_____

_____

_____

_____

God is a God of balance
Balance yourself

Spiritual – Today I will_____ to grow closer to God.

Mental – Today I will set my thoughts on_____.

Emotional – Today I will not be anxious about_____, but focus

on_____.

Physical – Today I will treat my body as a temple by_____.

Social – Today I will edify the body of Christ

by_____.

DAY TWENTY

SITTING WELL AT THE WELL

Satan's Lies	*God's Truths*
_____	_____
_____	_____
_____	_____
_____	_____
_____	_____

Defense Strategies

Positioning Yourself by pursuing God's Will

Who – Who is God using in my life?

_____

_____

What – What is God doing around me?

_____

_____

Where – Where do I see God most evident?

_____

_____

When – When do I feel most filled with the Fruits of the Spirit; peace, joy, love, gentleness, kindness, goodness, self-control, patience, and faithfulness

_____

_____

Armor of God

Armor Yourself

Belt of Truth - The truths God has revealed to me today

_____

_____

Breastplate of Righteousness – How has the Blood of Christ washed me clean?

_____

_____

Shoes of Peace – How has God reminded me that the battle is won?

_____

_____

Shield of Faith – How has God, in the past, rose beauty from ashes and restored what the locusts have eaten?

_____

_____

Helmet of Salvation – Who did Christ die for?

_____

_____

Sword of the Spirit – What verses or Bible stories has the Holy Spirit brought to mind to cut through the lies?

_____

_____

Prayer – My prayer today

_____

_____

_____

_____

God is a God of balance

Balance yourself

Spiritual – Today I will_____ to grow closer to God.

Mental – Today I will set my thoughts on_____.

Emotional – Today I will not be anxious about_____, but focus

on_____.

Physical – Today I will treat my body as a temple by_____.

Social – Today I will edify the body of Christ

by_____.

* * *

DAY TWENTY–ONE
SITTING WELL AT THE WELL

Satan's Lies

_____
_____
_____
_____

God's Truths

_____
_____
_____
_____

Defense Strategies
Positioning Yourself by pursuing God's Will

Who – Who is God using in my life?
_____
_____

What – What is God doing around me?
_____
_____

Where – Where do I see God most evident?
_____
_____

When – When do I feel most filled with the Fruits of the Spirit; peace, joy, love, gentleness, kindness, goodness, self-control, patience, and faithfulness
_____
_____

Armor of God
Armor Yourself

Belt of Truth - The truths God has revealed to me today
_____
_____

Breastplate of Righteousness – How has the Blood of Christ washed me clean?

_____

_____

Shoes of Peace – How has God reminded me that the battle is won?

_____

_____

Shield of Faith – How has God, in the past, rose beauty from ashes and restored what the locusts have eaten?

_____

_____

Helmet of Salvation – Who did Christ die for?

_____

_____

Sword of the Spirit – What verses or Bible stories has the Holy Spirit brought to mind to cut through the lies?

_____

_____

Prayer – My prayer today

_____

_____

_____

_____

God is a God of balance
Balance yourself

Spiritual – Today I will_____ to grow closer to God.

Mental – Today I will set my thoughts on_____.

Emotional – Today I will not be anxious about_____, but focus

on_____.

Physical – Today I will treat my body as a temple by_____.

Social – Today I will edify the body of Christ

by_____.

DAY TWENTY–TWO
SITTING WELL AT THE WELL

Satan's Lies   *God's Truths*

_____   _____

_____   _____

_____   _____

_____   _____

_____   _____

Defense Strategies

Positioning Yourself by pursuing God's Will

Who – Who is God using in my life?

_____

What – What is God doing around me?

_____

Where – Where do I see God most evident?

_____

When – When do I feel most filled with the Fruits of the Spirit; peace, joy, love, gentleness, kindness, goodness, self-control, patience, and faithfulness

_____

_____

Armor of God

Armor Yourself

Belt of Truth - The truths God has revealed to me today

_____

_____

Breastplate of Righteousness – How has the Blood of Christ washed me clean?

_____

_____

Shoes of Peace – How has God reminded me that the battle is won?

_____

_____

Shield of Faith – How has God, in the past, rose beauty from ashes and restored what the locusts have eaten?

_____

_____

Helmet of Salvation – Who did Christ die for?

_____

_____

Sword of the Spirit – What verses or Bible stories has the Holy Spirit brought to mind to cut through the lies?

_____

_____

Prayer – My prayer today

_____

_____

_____

_____

God is a God of balance

Balance yourself

Spiritual – Today I will_____ to grow closer to God.

Mental – Today I will set my thoughts on_____.

Emotional – Today I will not be anxious about_____, but focus on_____.

Physical – Today I will treat my body as a temple by_____.

Social – Today I will edify the body of Christ by_____.

DR. JEANNE BROOKS

✳ ✳ ✳

DAY TWENTY–THREE
SITTING WELL AT THE WELL

Satan's Lies   *God's Truths*

_____   _____
_____   _____

_____   _____

_____   _____

_____   _____

Defense Strategies

Positioning Yourself by pursuing God's Will

Who – Who is God using in my life?

_____

_____

What – What is God doing around me?

_____

_____

Where – Where do I see God most evident?

_____

_____

When – When do I feel most filled with the Fruits of the Spirit; peace, joy, love, gentleness, kindness, goodness, self-control, patience, and faithfulness

_____

_____

Armor of God

Armor Yourself

Belt of Truth - The truths God has revealed to me today

_____

_____

Breastplate of Righteousness – How has the Blood of Christ washed me clean?

_____

_____

Shoes of Peace – How has God reminded me that the battle is won?

_____

_____

Shield of Faith – How has God, in the past, rose beauty from ashes and restored what the locusts have eaten?

_____

_____

Helmet of Salvation – Who did Christ die for?

_____

_____

Sword of the Spirit – What verses or Bible stories has the Holy Spirit brought to mind to cut through the lies?

_____

_____

Prayer – My prayer today

_____

_____

_____

_____

God is a God of balance

Balance yourself

Spiritual – Today I will_____ to grow closer to God.

Mental – Today I will set my thoughts on_____.

Emotional – Today I will not be anxious about_____, but focus

on_____.

Physical – Today I will treat my body as a temple by_____.

Social – Today I will edify the body of Christ

by_____.

* * *

DAY TWENTY–FOUR
SITTING WELL AT THE WELL

Satan's Lies	*God's Truths*
_____	_____
_____	_____
_____	_____
_____	_____
_____	_____

Defense Strategies

Positioning Yourself by pursuing God's Will

Who – Who is God using in my life?

What – What is God doing around me?

Where – Where do I see God most evident?

When – When do I feel most filled with the Fruits of the Spirit; peace, joy, love, gentleness, kindness, goodness, self-control, patience, and faithfulness

Armor of God

Armor Yourself

Belt of Truth - The truths God has revealed to me today

Breastplate of Righteousness – How has the Blood of Christ washed me clean?

_____

_____

Shoes of Peace – How has God reminded me that the battle is won?

_____

_____

Shield of Faith – How has God, in the past, rose beauty from ashes and restored what the locusts have eaten?

_____

_____

Helmet of Salvation – Who did Christ die for?

_____

_____

Sword of the Spirit – What verses or Bible stories has the Holy Spirit brought to mind to cut through the lies?

_____

_____

Prayer – My prayer today

_____

_____

_____

_____

God is a God of balance
Balance yourself

Spiritual – Today I will_____ to grow closer to God.

Mental – Today I will set my thoughts on_____.

Emotional – Today I will not be anxious about_____, but focus on_____.

Physical – Today I will treat my body as a temple by_____.

Social – Today I will edify the body of Christ by_____.

DR. JEANNE BROOKS

DAY TWENTY–FIVE
SITTING WELL AT THE WELL

Satan's Lies   *God's Truths*

_____   _____
_____   _____
_____   _____
_____   _____
_____   _____

Defense Strategies
Positioning Yourself by pursuing God's Will

Who – Who is God using in my life?

_____

_____

What – What is God doing around me?

_____

_____

Where – Where do I see God most evident?

_____

_____

When – When do I feel most filled with the Fruits of the Spirit; peace, joy, love, gentleness, kindness, goodness, self-control, patience, and faithfulness

_____

_____

Armor of God
Armor Yourself

Belt of Truth - The truths God has revealed to me today

_____

_____

Breastplate of Righteousness – How has the Blood of Christ washed me clean?

_____

_____

Shoes of Peace – How has God reminded me that the battle is won?

_____

_____

Shield of Faith – How has God, in the past, rose beauty from ashes and restored what the locusts have eaten?

_____

_____

Helmet of Salvation – Who did Christ die for?

_____

_____

Sword of the Spirit – What verses or Bible stories has the Holy Spirit brought to mind to cut through the lies?

_____

_____

Prayer – My prayer today

_____

_____

_____

_____

God is a God of balance
Balance yourself

Spiritual – Today I will_____ to grow closer to God.

Mental – Today I will set my thoughts on_____.

Emotional – Today I will not be anxious about_____, but focus

on_____.

Physical – Today I will treat my body as a temple by_____.

Social – Today I will edify the body of Christ

by_____.

* * *

DAY TWENTY–SIX
SITTING WELL AT THE WELL

Satan's Lies   *God's Truths*

_____   _____
_____   _____
_____   _____
_____   _____
_____   _____

Defense Strategies
Positioning Yourself by pursuing God's Will

Who – Who is God using in my life?
_____

What – What is God doing around me?
_____

Where – Where do I see God most evident?
_____

When – When do I feel most filled with the Fruits of the Spirit; peace, joy, love, gentleness, kindness, goodness, self-control, patience, and faithfulness
_____
_____

Armor of God
Armor Yourself

Belt of Truth - The truths God has revealed to me today
_____
_____

Breastplate of Righteousness – How has the Blood of Christ washed me clean?

_____

_____

Shoes of Peace – How has God reminded me that the battle is won?

_____

_____

Shield of Faith – How has God, in the past, rose beauty from ashes and restored what the locusts have eaten?

_____

_____

Helmet of Salvation – Who did Christ die for?

_____

_____

Sword of the Spirit – What verses or Bible stories has the Holy Spirit brought to mind to cut through the lies?

_____

_____

Prayer – My prayer today

_____

_____

_____

_____

God is a God of balance
Balance yourself

Spiritual – Today I will_____ to grow closer to God.

Mental – Today I will set my thoughts on_____.

Emotional – Today I will not be anxious about_____, but focus on_____.

Physical – Today I will treat my body as a temple by_____.

Social – Today I will edify the body of Christ by_____.

* * *

DAY TWENTY-SEVEN
SITTING WELL AT THE WELL

Satan's Lies	*God's Truths*
_____	_____
_____	_____
_____	_____
_____	_____
_____	_____

Defense Strategies
Positioning Yourself by pursuing God's Will

Who – Who is God using in my life?

_____

_____

What – What is God doing around me?

_____

_____

Where – Where do I see God most evident?

_____

_____

When – When do I feel most filled with the Fruits of the Spirit; peace, joy, love, gentleness, kindness, goodness, self-control, patience, and faithfulness

_____

_____

Armor of God
Armor Yourself

Belt of Truth - The truths God has revealed to me today

_____

Breastplate of Righteousness – How has the Blood of Christ washed me clean?

_____

_____

Shoes of Peace – How has God reminded me that the battle is won?

_____

_____

Shield of Faith – How has God, in the past, rose beauty from ashes and restored what the locusts have eaten?

_____

_____

Helmet of Salvation – Who did Christ die for?

_____

_____

Sword of the Spirit – What verses or Bible stories has the Holy Spirit brought to mind to cut through the lies?

_____

_____

Prayer – My prayer today

_____

_____

_____

_____

God is a God of balance

Balance yourself

Spiritual – Today I will_____ to grow closer to God.

Mental – Today I will set my thoughts on_____.

Emotional – Today I will not be anxious about_____, but focus

on_____.

Physical – Today I will treat my body as a temple by_____.

Social – Today I will edify the body of Christ

by_____.

* * *

DAY TWENTY–EIGHT
SITTING WELL AT THE WELL

Satan's Lies   *God's Truths*

_____   _____

_____   _____

_____   _____

_____   _____

_____   _____

Defense Strategies

Positioning Yourself by pursuing God's Will

Who – Who is God using in my life?

_____

What – What is God doing around me?

_____

Where – Where do I see God most evident?

_____

When – When do I feel most filled with the Fruits of the Spirit; peace, joy, love, gentleness, kindness, goodness, self-control, patience, and faithfulness

_____

_____

Armor of God

Armor Yourself

Belt of Truth - The truths God has revealed to me today

_____

Breastplate of Righteousness – How has the Blood of Christ washed me clean?

_____

_____

Shoes of Peace – How has God reminded me that the battle is won?

_____

_____

Shield of Faith – How has God, in the past, rose beauty from ashes and restored what the locusts have eaten?

_____

_____

Helmet of Salvation – Who did Christ die for?

_____

_____

Sword of the Spirit – What verses or Bible stories has the Holy Spirit brought to mind to cut through the lies?

_____

_____

Prayer – My prayer today

_____

_____

_____

_____

God is a God of balance
Balance yourself

Spiritual – Today I will_____ to grow closer to God.

Mental – Today I will set my thoughts on_____.

Emotional – Today I will not be anxious about_____, but focus on_____.

Physical – Today I will treat my body as a temple by_____.

Social – Today I will edify the body of Christ by_____.

* * *

DAY TWENTY-NINE
SITTING WELL AT THE WELL

Satan's Lies	*God's Truths*
_____	_____
_____	_____
_____	_____
_____	_____
_____	_____

Defense Strategies

Positioning Yourself by pursuing God's Will

Who – Who is God using in my life?

_____

_____

What – What is God doing around me?

_____

_____

Where – Where do I see God most evident?

_____

_____

When – When do I feel most filled with the Fruits of the Spirit; peace, joy, love, gentleness, kindness, goodness, self-control, patience, and faithfulness

_____

_____

Armor of God

Armor Yourself

Belt of Truth - The truths God has revealed to me today

_____

_____

Breastplate of Righteousness – How has the Blood of Christ washed me clean?

_____

_____

Shoes of Peace – How has God reminded me that the battle is won?

_____

_____

Shield of Faith – How has God, in the past, rose beauty from ashes and restored what the locusts have eaten?

_____

_____

Helmet of Salvation – Who did Christ die for?

_____

_____

Sword of the Spirit – What verses or Bible stories has the Holy Spirit brought to mind to cut through the lies?

_____

_____

Prayer – My prayer today

_____

_____

_____

_____

God is a God of balance
Balance yourself

Spiritual – Today I will_____ to grow closer to God.

Mental – Today I will set my thoughts on_____.

Emotional – Today I will not be anxious about_____, but focus

on_____.

Physical – Today I will treat my body as a temple by_____.

Social – Today I will edify the body of Christ

by_____.

DAY THIRTY

SITTING WELL AT THE WELL

Satan's Lies

_____

_____

_____

_____

_____

God's Truths

_____

_____

_____

_____

_____

Defense Strategies

Positioning Yourself by pursuing God's Will

Who – Who is God using in my life?

_____

_____

What – What is God doing around me?

_____

_____

Where – Where do I see God most evident?

_____

_____

When – When do I feel most filled with the Fruits of the Spirit; peace, joy, love, gentleness, kindness, goodness, self-control, patience, and faithfulness

_____

_____

Armor of God

Armor Yourself

Belt of Truth - The truths God has revealed to me today

_____

Breastplate of Righteousness – How has the Blood of Christ washed me clean?

_____

_____

Shoes of Peace – How has God reminded me that the battle is won?

_____

_____

Shield of Faith – How has God, in the past, rose beauty from ashes and restored what the locusts have eaten?

_____

_____

Helmet of Salvation – Who did Christ die for?

_____

_____

Sword of the Spirit – What verses or Bible stories has the Holy Spirit brought to mind to cut through the lies?

_____

_____

Prayer – My prayer today

_____

_____

_____

_____

God is a God of balance
Balance yourself

Spiritual – Today I will_____ to grow closer to God.

Mental – Today I will set my thoughts on_____.

Emotional – Today I will not be anxious about_____, but focus on_____.

Physical – Today I will treat my body as a temple by_____.

Social – Today I will edify the body of Christ by_____.

* * *

About the Author

Dr. Jeanne Brooks has a PhD in psychology working in the field for over twenty-five years. She had a private practice with the Samaritan Counseling Center of East Texas with her specialty areas working with troubled adolescents, alcohol and drug addiction, as well as helping children and families adjust to divorce. Dr. Brooks worked in local schools providing programming for alcohol/drug abuse and violence prevention. She worked closely with the local Juvenile Probation Office providing parenting, alcohol and drug abuse, and healthy coping groups. Finally, she worked closely with the Courts in her area and surrounding counties providing mental health assessments, referral, and treatment services for children and parents adjusting to divorce. Her passion clearly has been working in crisis care with children. She moved to Lynchburg Virginia in the summer of 2008 to begin teaching graduate and PhD students' clinical skills. She currently is a full-time faculty member for the Center for Counselor Education and family Studies department at Liberty University and has a part time private practice with Advanced Psychotherapeutics.

www.DrJeanneBrooks.com

Made in the USA
Columbia, SC
24 February 2018